"WHEN
DESTINY CALLS . . .

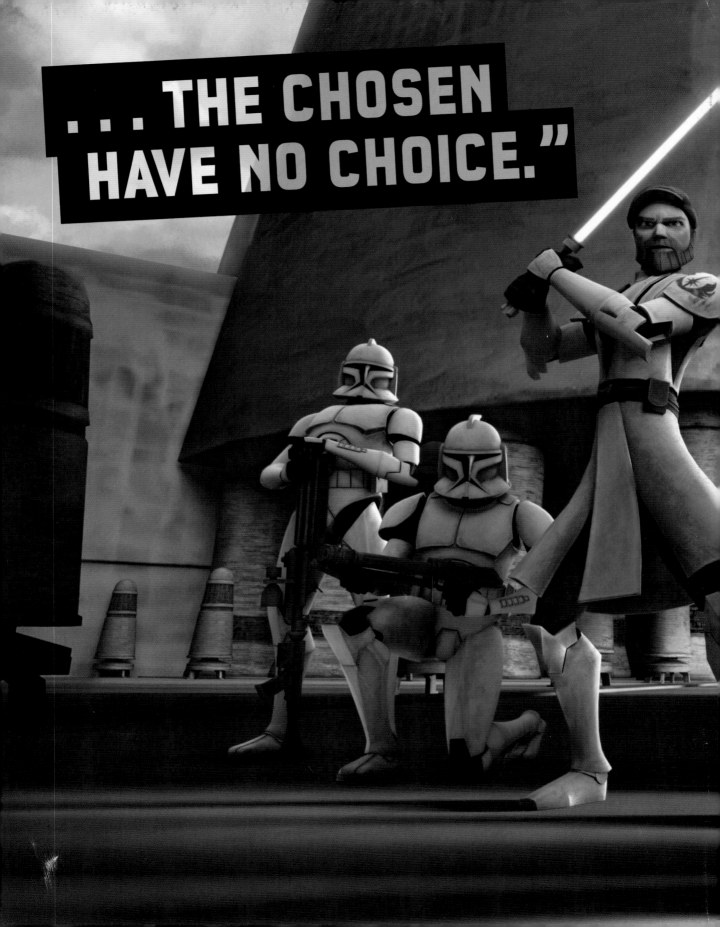

WHO ARE THE JEDI?

**WRITTEN BY
GLENN DAKIN**

CONTENTS

TIMELINE

The Clone Wars take place in a time between 22 BBY and 19 BBY (BBY stands for Before the Battle of Yavin). More information about this period is still coming to light, but the timeline shows some of the important events in the Clone Wars known to date.

22 BBY

Battle of Christophsis

First Battle of Geonosis

Sky Battle of Quell

Second Battle of Geonosis

WHAT ARE THE CLONE WARS?

A galaxy divided! After years of peace under the rule of the Republic, war is spreading among the planets. The Separatists, led by Count Dooku, want to tear the old order apart and gain power from war. They have greedy allies, including the Trade Federation and the Techno Union, who provide credits, spaceships, and most of all, legions of deadly droids to drive on the war effort.

The old Republic, ruled by Chancellor Palpatine, is defended by the Jedi and a vast army of clone troopers. The Republic forces seek to stop the Separatist forces from invading neutral planets. Unknown to the Jedi, the war is really being controlled by the Sith Lord Darth Sidious, whose mission is to create chaos in the galaxy so that the dark side of the Force can dominate it.

Battle of
Malastare

Battle of
Umbara

19 BBY

Battle of
Ryloth

Battle of
Kamino

Battle of
Mon Cala

Separatist
massacre of
Nightsisters

WHAT IS A CLONE TROOPER?

Clone troopers are bred with a built-in sense of duty. They become fully grown, fully trained soldiers for the Republic's Grand Army in just 10 years. Each clone trooper is an exact copy of Jango Fett, a military expert and ace bounty hunter who helped set up the cloning program.

WHO ARE THE JEDI?

The Jedi are an ancient order who use the Force to fight evil. They are known as the peacekeepers of the galaxy—but when war erupts, they must become soldiers instead. As the Separatists seek to break up the old Republic, Jedi generals lead vast clone armies against Count Dooku and his droids.

THE JEDI COUNCIL

Twelve wise Jedi Masters, known as the Jedi Council, make important decisions about war matters. Led by Yoda, they meet at the Jedi Temple on the planet Coruscant. The Jedi Council discuss their decisions with the leader of the Republic, Chancellor Palpatine, before acting.

LIGHTSABER FORCE

The main weapon of the Jedi is the lightsaber, a beam of plasma that can slice through almost anything. They use their lightsabers with skill and restraint, never anger. Every Jedi guards his or her lightsaber well because their life depends on it.

CLONE FORCE

The Republic has created a vast army of clones to fight in the war alongside the Jedi. The bond between the clone troopers and their Jedi generals is very strong. The Jedi lay their lives on the line for their men, and the clones will follow a Jedi into any peril.

The Jedi Code sets out the ideas that Jedi live by. Peace, discipline, and the Force are key.

WHAT MAKES YODA A GOOD LEADER OF THE JEDI?

The Jedi are the most powerful warriors in the galaxy. Because they are unique, it takes someone very special to be their Grand Master—a Jedi with a rare combination of skills. Yoda is that person, but what makes him right for the job?

He Is A Motivator
Yoda inspires loyalty in those who follow him. On a successful mission to fight battle droids on the moon of Rugosa, he asks his army of clone troopers to take off their helmets. Although they all look the same, he tells them, they are all very different in the Force.

STAFF DOUBLES AS A WEAPON.

WHO IS YODA?

Yoda is the most famous Jedi of all, known and respected across the galaxy. No one has a greater knowledge of the Force or its strength and dangers. Like a wise father, Yoda guides his Jedi Knights from afar. Using the Force, he can send his thoughts into their minds.

He Is Wise

Yoda considers every path and outcome, and never seeks glory in battle—only a way toward peace. He is never controlled by anger, greed, or revenge. He also listens to trusted friends, such as Mace Windu, before he acts.

TRUE OR FALSE?

Yoda is known to be the last of his race.

False: Yoda's race is unknown, but there are more of his kind.

He Is Skilled

The most skilled of all Jedi with a lightsaber, Yoda is perhaps the only one who can outdo Count Dooku in a duel. He fights with amazing speed and agility using the Ataru lightsaber style, which involves mid-air spins and acrobatic Force leaps.

WHAT IS THE FORCE?

An invisible energy known as the Force flows through everything in the galaxy. There are two sides to the Force—dark and light—and the Jedi only ever use the light side. Its powers can be used in many different ways—as a weapon, a helpful tool, or a form of communication. It can even save lives . . . and also end them.

HOLO DATA

To the Jedi, the Force is not just a source of power—it is a vital connection between all living things and the galaxy as a whole. Learning to be in tune with the Force is a way of life.

Mind Power

A Jedi can use the Force to influence the minds of their foes. Some Jedi can speak mind-to-mind, using telepathy. Through meditation, Jedi can sense danger and sometimes see into the future.

Force Field

With a focused mind, a Jedi can use the Force to create a shield. This can hold back deadly gas, push away an adversary, and even deflect enemy droids or weapon fire.

Force Leaps

With the Force behind them, Jedi can leap great distances. A Force leap can turn even a small Jedi such as Yoda into a much more powerful opponent.

Levitation

The more a Jedi is in tune with the Force, the more impressive are his feats of power. Anakin can move hunks of debris or massive rocks, either to turn them into weapons or to save lives.

WHAT IS THE DARK SIDE?

If the light side of the Force brings harmony to the galaxy, then the dark side brings the opposite. The Sith are masters of the dark side, which believes in passion over calm, violence over peace. Its followers are prepared to use hate, greed, and fear to obtain whatever they want.

FORCE LIGHTNING

One of the deadliest weapons of the dark side is Force lightning, a way of channeling the Force through your hands to electrocute your foe. Skilled Jedi can learn to deflect this back at the attacker.

DESTRUCTIVE MIND

The dark side can make people feel superior to ordinary mortals. They become cruel and aloof, forgetting the value of life. When Jedi Pong Krell falls to the dark side, he begins to despise his own clone troopers, sending many to their deaths without a second thought.

TRUE OR FALSE?

The dark side of the Force is strongest.

False—however, the dark side is more tempting.

EVIL VISIONS

At a time of crisis in an individual's life, the dark side can cause shadowy visions to cloud the mind, bringing forbidden knowledge of the future. Anakin sees dark images of losing his humanity when he visits the Well of the Dark Side on the planet Mortis, where the dark side is at its strongest. Anakin will be a force for evil indeed, if he should ever fall to the dark side.

TWIN BLADES

Are two blades better than one? In the Jar'Kai style of combat, a fighter wields either two lightsabers at once or a staff which has been split in two. An expert like Asajj Ventress can use the twin blades to create a Rising Whirlwind attack, spinning them around like an unstoppable tornado.

WHAT IS A LIGHTSABER?

An ancient weapon with a glowing blade, the lightsaber makes an unforgettable sound as it cuts through the air. It will forever be linked with the Jedi, who each build their own lightsaber and use it to battle in their own unique way. However, the Sith use lightsabers, too. They wield their destructive power with more venom, but less artistry.

LIGHTSABER

GREEN PLASMA BLADE

A lightsaber consists of a hilt and a plasma blade. Inside the hilt is a power cell that heats up plasma gas to create the blade, and a crystal that gives it color and length. Controls on the side set the power level.

- **TYPE** MELEE WEAPON (HAND WEAPON)
- **LENGTH** 20–30 CM (8–12 IN)
- **MANUFACTURE** OWNER-MADE

LIGHTSABER HILT

KIT FISTO'S LIGHTSABER

PLO KOON'S LIGHTSABER

YODA'S LIGHTSABER

COMBAT STYLES

There are seven styles of lightsaber combat. One of the most spectacular is Ataru, which is also known as the Way of the Hawk-Bat. It combines lightsaber skill with Force-assisted leaps, and involves the pre-jump crouch stance. Yoda is an expert in Ataru.

DARKSABER

The darksaber is a long-lost Jedi weapon. It was stolen from the Jedi centuries ago and passed on to Pre Vizsla, leader of the Death Watch terror group. It has a flatter, sharper blade than a lightsaber, but its powers are as yet unknown.

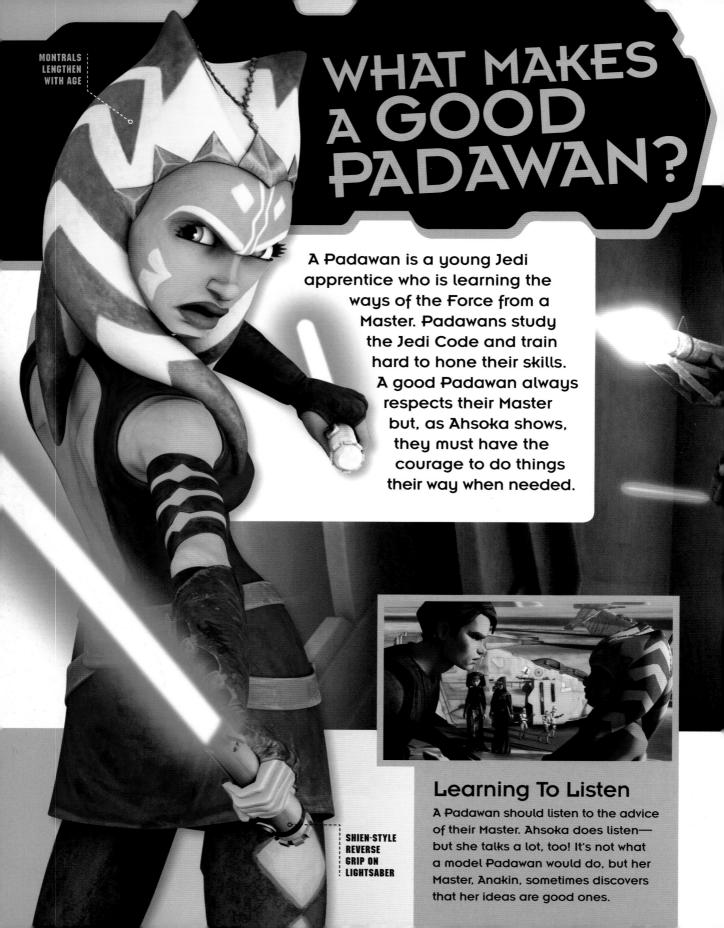

MONTRALS LENGTHEN WITH AGE

WHAT MAKES A GOOD PADAWAN?

A Padawan is a young Jedi apprentice who is learning the ways of the Force from a Master. Padawans study the Jedi Code and train hard to hone their skills. A good Padawan always respects their Master but, as Ahsoka shows, they must have the courage to do things their way when needed.

SHIEN-STYLE REVERSE GRIP ON LIGHTSABER

Learning To Listen

A Padawan should listen to the advice of their Master. Ahsoka does listen—but she talks a lot, too! It's not what a model Padawan would do, but her Master, Anakin, sometimes discovers that her ideas are good ones.

Learning Teamwork

No matter how great a Padawan's skills, they will always achieve more if they learn to work as part of a team. A watchful Padawan knows when to cover their Master's back in battle, and when to take the lead. Ahsoka and Anakin quickly develop a kind of telepathy, each knowing what the other is going to do—most of the time.

HOLO DATA

Ahsoka is a Togruta, a species from the planet Shili. Like all Togrutas, she has head-tails and horns called montrals that help her to sense the movements of objects close by.

WHO IS AHSOKA?

Ahsoka Tano is a daring young Padawan. Anakin calls her "Snips" because she is often snippy with him! Nevertheless, the two have formed a close bond. Ahsoka is already skilled with the Force. She can perform Force leaps and once even used the Force to pull down a wall.

Learning Battle Skills

A good Padawan learns to use their special strengths. Ahsoka is light, fast, and agile. She is also brave to the point of foolishness sometimes, which can be a good or bad thing! Taking big risks can turn a battle around, but it can sometimes put others in danger.

The Sith Lord known as Darth Sidious is the leader of the Sith, but his true identity is a secret. When he wishes to speak with his Sith apprentice, Count Dooku, he only ever does so via hologram.

The Sith

The ancient order of the Sith follow the dark side of the Force. They seek to rule the galaxy through tyranny and fear, using the power of hatred and greed to control people. The Jedi, sworn to protecting the innocent from harm, are their natural enemies in an eternal battle for the cosmos.

WHO ARE THE ENEMIES OF THE JEDI?

The Jedi do not seek enemies, yet they attract them all the same! Some attack the Jedi in return for payment. Others make money from war, and hate peace-makers. Worst of all are those who wish to see the galaxy plunged into darkness and chaos . . .

Bounty Hunters

As war spreads, law and order breaks down in the galaxy. This is great news for bounty hunters such as Cad Bane, who hire themselves out to crime lords to destroy or kidnap the Jedi and other targets, plunder, or do any other dirty jobs. Rewards for capturing a Jedi are high indeed!

The Techno Union

The Techno Union is an alliance of business corporations that build weapons, battleships, and droids to sell on to the Separatists. The longer the fighting continues, the more profit they make, so they actively seek to keep the war going for as long as possible and despise the Jedi for their efforts to stop it. Wat Tambor, foreman of the Techno Union, joins Count Dooku in creating conflict wherever he can.

WHY IS ANAKIN A GREAT JEDI?

There are many brave Jedi warriors battling the dark side forces, yet Anakin Skywalker has been called the greatest of them all. He has survived impossible odds in war and triumphed against fearsome foes. What qualities make Anakin a great hero? And is there a side to Anakin that is not so great?

MECHANICAL FOREARM AND HAND

He Is Strong-Willed

Anakin is a natural winner who does not back down and never makes excuses. If he can see a way to win a battle, he will do it, regardless of the risk to himself. But Yoda can sometimes see danger in Anakin's bold attitude, so he gives Anakin a Padawan to help teach him how to control his feelings and how to let things go.

LIGHT JEDI ROBE AIDS AGILITY

SINGLE BLADE, FORM V STANCE

He Is Loyal

Freed from slavery by a Jedi Master at a young age, Anakin has always been loyal to the Jedi Order. For years he has never questioned their wisdom, or that of Palpatine. But war makes him see differently. He learns that the strict Jedi Code can hold a warrior back from victory.

HOLO DATA

Anakin is a human from the desert planet of Tatooine, where he lived until he was nine as a slave along with his mother, Shmi. Of all the Jedi, Anakin has the highest recorded level of the Force.

He Is Strong In The Force

Anakin's strength in the Force makes him an awesome starfighter pilot, and he can also use Force leaps and the Force push to great effect. However, he is yet to learn how to make full use of his ability.

WHO IS ANAKIN?

Anakin Skywalker is a brave Jedi general, loved by his clone troopers and feared by his foes. Some believe he is the Chosen One, who will one day bring balance to the Force. He has a difficult path ahead, including a battle with the dark side of the Force.

25

WHO FIGHTS ALONGSIDE THE JEDI?

The Jedi are not short of allies in their battle with the Separatists. Some are born for the job, like the clone troopers. Some are built for it, like the droids. Others are aliens who share Jedi ideals. But all of them know that the galaxy would be a dark place without the Jedi.

Clone Troopers

Clone troopers are bred on the planet Kamino with one purpose—to aid the Republic in the war. Millions of clone troopers form the Republic's Grand Army, commanded by Chancellor Palpatine, which battles the Separatists under the leadership of Jedi generals.

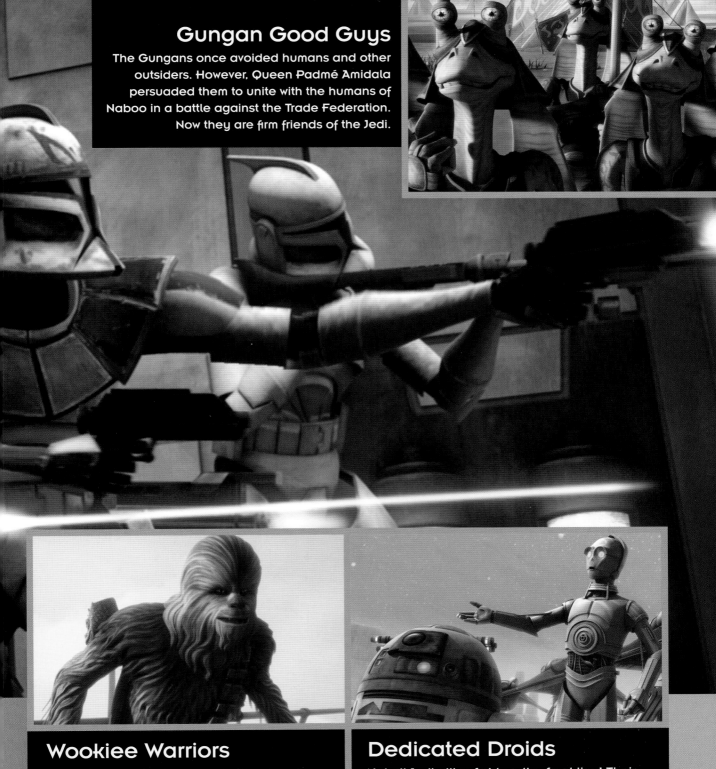

Gungan Good Guys

The Gungans once avoided humans and other outsiders. However, Queen Padmé Amidala persuaded them to unite with the humans of Naboo in a battle against the Trade Federation. Now they are firm friends of the Jedi.

Wookiee Warriors

Brave, immensely strong, and with a knack for fixing things, Wookiees are loyal friends to the Jedi and valuable allies in battle. Wookiees stayed out of the Clone Wars at first. That changed when the Separatists began to seek control of their planet, Kashyyyk, and tried to take over their hyperspace lanes.

Dedicated Droids

Not all Jedi allies fight on the front line! Their army of trusty droids carries out countless tasks for the war effort. It includes astromech droids like R2-D2, who tirelessly maintain the Jedi warships, and protocol droids like C-3PO, who perform tricky translations under enemy fire with unfailing politeness.

SHOULD YOU JUDGE A JEDI'S SHIP BY THE WAY IT LOOKS?

Anakin Skywalker is one of the best pilots in the Jedi fleet—some say the very best. Any ship he chooses as his personal favorite has to be something special. A humble freighter, the *Twilight* may look like a small, meteor-scarred pile of junk, but under its bumps and scratches it is full of surprises.

HIDDEN EXTRAS

Lacking style on the outside and shiny tech on the inside, the *Twilight* looks like the most basic craft around. Don't be fooled! It is fitted with an array of hidden missile launchers and laser cannons which are operated from the cockpit.

FAST AND NIMBLE

Despite its clumsy appearance, the *Twilight* is fast and nimble—great for dodging enemy guns and making fast getaways. Small in size, it slips easily through enemy lines. Anakin has souped up the engine to ensure a quick jump into hyperspace.

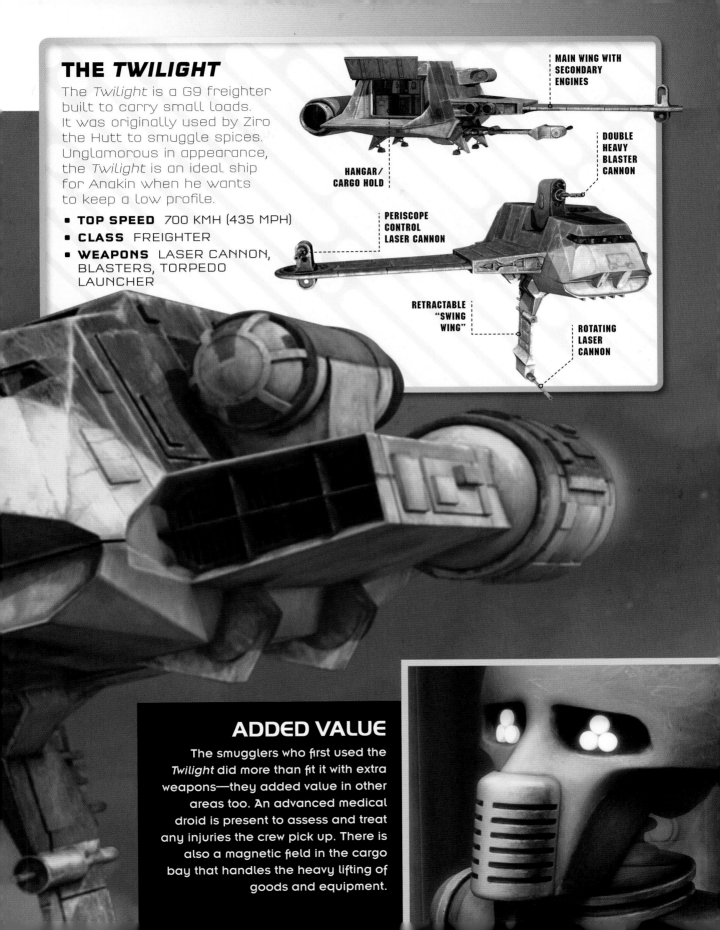

THE *TWILIGHT*

The *Twilight* is a G9 freighter built to carry small loads. It was originally used by Ziro the Hutt to smuggle spices. Unglamorous in appearance, the *Twilight* is an ideal ship for Anakin when he wants to keep a low profile.

- **TOP SPEED** 700 KMH (435 MPH)
- **CLASS** FREIGHTER
- **WEAPONS** LASER CANNON, BLASTERS, TORPEDO LAUNCHER

MAIN WING WITH SECONDARY ENGINES

DOUBLE HEAVY BLASTER CANNON

HANGAR/ CARGO HOLD

PERISCOPE CONTROL LASER CANNON

RETRACTABLE "SWING WING"

ROTATING LASER CANNON

ADDED VALUE

The smugglers who first used the *Twilight* did more than fit it with extra weapons—they added value in other areas too. An advanced medical droid is present to assess and treat any injuries the crew pick up. There is also a magnetic field in the cargo bay that handles the heavy lifting of goods and equipment.

WHAT MAKES R2-D2 A GREAT FRIEND?

HOLO PROJECTOR

MAIN SENSOR

All droids are helpful; that is their function. But some droids seem to go way beyond their programming. R2-D2 is a little astromech droid with a big personality that makes him not just a helper, but a true friend to many.

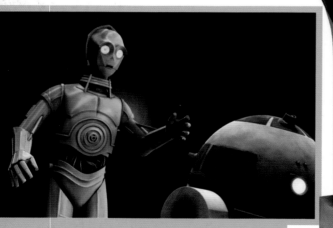

He Solves Problems

R2-D2 is a natural problem-solver and a perfect ally in a tight spot. He is the ideal friend for C-3PO, who often gets into a pickle! While C-3PO panics, R2-D2 gets to work finding the quickest way out of danger.

He Is Very Loyal

R2-D2 is a loyal friend to Anakin, and R2's loyalty is repaid. Anakin risks his own life to rescue R2 when he falls into the hands of deadly cyborg General Grievous. R2's quirky personality is actually down to Anakin—it is caused by an overload of data because Anakin refuses to wipe his memory!

WHO IS R2-D2?

R2-D2's many years of service have made him a brave and resourceful astromech droid. His small body contains an amazing box of tricks that he uses to defend himself when he finds himself in trouble. They include a buzz-saw, electric pike, and oil injector.

HOLO DATA

R2-D2 was built by a company called Industrial Automaton. His main duties are helping to pilot starfighters and fixing machinery. R2 stands at half the height of Anakin.

He Is Fearless

Despite being short of real weapons, R2 never runs from a fight and is always ready to face all kinds of danger to help his friends. When faced with a snarling gundark, he tries every gadget he has to fend off its jaws. R2 has also taken on bounty hunters, battle droids, and even an almighty Zillo Beast.

HOW DO THE JEDI DESTROY THE MALEVOLENCE?

The *Malevolence* is a massive battleship built to strike dread into the hearts of Count Dooku's enemies. Its twin ion cannons can wipe out whole fleets of enemy ships. With the merciless General Grievous as its commander, the ship is a weapon of fear that the Jedi must somehow stop.

THE *MALEVOLENCE*

The *Malevolence* is a *Subjugator*-class heavy cruiser. Its defenses include long-range turbolasers and cannons for taking out starfighters. It also has a powerful tractor beam to draw careless visitors into its hold.

- **CLASS** DREADNOUGHT
- **LENGTH** 4,845 M (15,895 FT)
- **CREW** 900 (DROIDS)

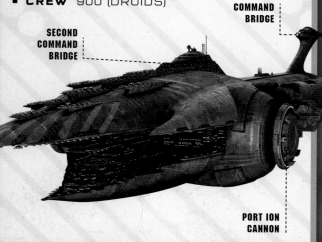

SECOND COMMAND BRIDGE

COMMAND BRIDGE

PORT ION CANNON

THEY ASSESS THEIR TARGET

The *Malevolence* is too well defended to be taken down by Republic cruisers. Anakin makes a bold decision to take smaller Y-wing fighters in close and attack Grievous on his battle bridge. This brave approach soon gets them within striking distance.

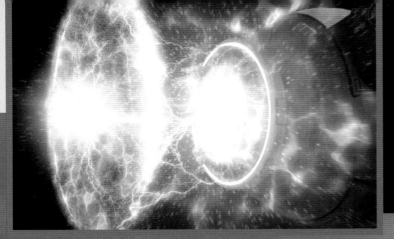

THEY ATTACK

Anakin soon realizes that his squadron will not survive the close-range attack, so he changes his plan and targets an ion cannon. It's in the process of recharging when it takes multiple hits from the Y-wings' proton torpedoes. When Grievous tries to power up the ion cannon, it overloads, wrecking his ship.

THEY SEIZE CONTROL

With the enemy ship damaged, the time has come to finish it off. Anakin sneaks aboard the *Twilight*, and, with the help of Padmé Amidala, takes over the navi-computer. He hot-wires the ship to take a new course when the hyperdrive is activated—and escapes before it flies into the nearest moon!

WHAT IS THE JEDI'S DEADLIEST

Using weapons with massive destructive power is not the Jedi way. But it is crucial that they win the war. When a Republic scientist invents an electro-proton bomb that can wipe out a whole droid army, Chancellor Palpatine expects the Jedi to use it. It could certainly save the lives of many clone troopers. The Jedi agree to try out the bomb, but some feel it will not bring a victory to be proud of.

THE BOMB

In this war, the enemy uses mostly droid soldiers. To take advantage of this fact, Republic weapons expert Dr. Sionver Boll creates a device that will harm only machines, not people. When dropped on a target, the bomb releases earth-shaking power.

HOLO DATA

The electro-proton bomb is a giant version of the EMP grenade regularly used by clone troopers. The grenade sends out a strong electro-magnetic pulse that switches off a droid's power.

WEAPON?

THE POWER

The ion-powered bomb sends out a massive pulse of energy that turns even the deadliest droid into a pile of scrap. A dome-shaped electron field covers the whole enemy army and sizzles every circuit. It also sends out a shock wave that sweeps droids away like a tsunami!

NO REFUSAL

Jedi Mace Windu resists using the bomb right up until the last moment, but Chancellor Palpatine forces him to agree. He says the bomb is now their only hope of winning the war. In the end, even Mace must accept the will of the leader of the Republic.

"I HAVE A BAD FEELING ABOUT THIS."
MACE WINDU

HOOD
RESTS ON
EYESTALKS

WHAT HAPPENS WHEN YOU IMPERSONATE A JEDI?

Pretending to be a Jedi is a tough challenge—and a dangerous one! You may have the courage but what you don't have on your side is the Force. Both Jar Jar Binks and the bounty hunter Cade Bane discover how perilous it can be to put on Jedi robes . . .

NABOO
SENATOR
ROBES

WHO IS JAR JAR?

A friendly Gungan with a habit of landing himself in danger, Jar Jar Binks is a junior senator, representing his homeworld Naboo, alongside Padmé Amidala. He has been a friend to the Jedi ever since his life was saved by one—Qui-Gon Jinn. Like all Gungans, he can breathe on land and water. He speaks a quirky version of Galactic Basic.

You Use Your Skills

Without the Force, Jar Jar must rely on his own skills when he dons Anakin's robe to save his friend, Padmé Amidala, from the enemy. She is being held on a swamp world like his own home. Jar Jar knows how to persuade swamp creatures, like this Kwazel Maw, to help him out.

You Get Into Trouble!

The Separatists will believe you are an incredibly powerful foe and send their deadliest forces to stop you. A battalion of battle droids is the least you can expect to face. It's a good job "Jedi" Jar Jar has a habit of making lucky escapes.

The Jedi Catch You

Bounty hunter Cad Bane disguises himself as a Jedi in order to kidnap a Jedi child. But the real Jedi are one step ahead of him—they use the Force to discover what Bane is up to and capture him in an ambush on Naboo.

HOLOCRON HIDEAWAY

Some secrets, such as the names of children gifted in the Force, could put innocents at risk if they ever made it into enemy hands. Jedi store confidential data like this in Holocrons—boxes that only a Jedi can open.

TEMPLE VAULT

Deep in the Jedi Temple is a guarded vault containing the most important secrets of the war. Here lie things that enemy eyes must never see, including codes to hidden hyperspace lanes, blueprints for secret weapons, and names of Jedi spies.

WHAT ARE THE GREATEST SECRETS OF THE JEDI?

Honesty is important to all Jedi. They believe that being open with others spreads friendship and understanding. But in a time of war, they must be careful. Some things must remain secrets. If not, they could put people in danger, or even change the whole course of the conflict . . .

HOLO DATA

Holocron is short for holographic chronicle. Once a Holocron is opened, you can speak with it and ask it questions. Holocrons can be unlocked by a Jedi using the Force and a unique crystal key.

FORBIDDEN SECRETS

Sometimes it is wrong to keep secrets. When Anakin Skywalker and Padmé Amidala marry, they keep it to themselves. But Jedi are not allowed such close attachments. If any harm comes to Padmé it could lead Anakin to despair—and to the dark side!

ULTIMATE SECRET

Some of the biggest secrets of the war are known only to the Jedi High Council. In a complex scheme, Obi-Wan Kenobi fakes his own death and then takes on the identity of his murderer to get behind enemy lines.

WHAT IS A FORCE-SENSITIVE SPACECRAFT?

Relying on technology can be frustrating for Jedi. Its complex systems and odd glitches can slow them down. But starfighters like the *Aethersprite* are different. This craft is Force-sensitive, so it becomes at one with the Jedi and allows them to act at the speed of thought.

HOLO DATA

The Jedi Starfighter Corps is a fleet of starfighters created by Jedi Master Saesee Tiin. Tiin works with star fliers such as Plo Koon and Anakin to train clone troopers to become ace pilots.

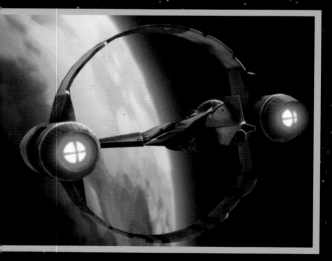

RING OF POWER

It is not the Force that sends a starfighter into hyperspace, it is a detachable booster called a hyperdrive ring. Once in hyperspace, which is a different dimension in space, a Force-sensitive spacecraft can travel at extremely fast speeds.

STRIKE FORCE

The starfighter is designed for swift military action. It has few shield powers, relying on its pilot to use the Force to move at the speed of thought and dodge enemy fire. A well-piloted craft can speed through an asteroid field or dangerous debris without even slowing down.

MECH MATE

Having an astromech co-pilot leaves the Jedi free to forget the technical stuff and just use the Force. Astromechs plot routes through hyperspace lanes, keep an eye on flight systems, and squeeze the best possible performance out of the craft.

DELTA-7B
AETHERSPRITE

The *Aethersprite* is a thin-hulled starfighter with systems that respond instantly to Jedi reflexes. A full-sized astromech droid fits in the droid socket in the hull, just ahead of the cockpit.

- **MODEL** LIGHT INTERCEPTOR
- **WEAPONS** LASER CANNONS (4)
- **SPEED** 1,250 KPH (777 MPH)
- **LENGTH** 8 M (26 FT)

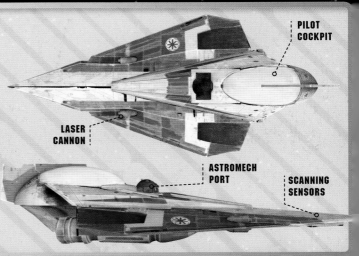

PILOT COCKPIT

LASER CANNON

ASTROMECH PORT

SCANNING SENSORS

DO JEDI PLANS EVER GO WRONG?

Jedi are famed for pulling off amazing feats, but they do not rely on luck. They plan every mission to the last detail, using Holonet maps to study their target and selecting the ideal team for the job. But even Jedi plans can go wrong. Inside an enemy prison, a Jedi rescue team find things don't go quite as they expected . . .

PRISON PLAN

Jedi Master Even Piell has vital information about the Nexus Route—secret hyperspace lanes that could help win the war. But he is being held in the enemy's high-security prison, the Citadel. A Jedi team sets off to rescue Piell, using re-programmed battle droids as pilots.

"BRING OUT THE ANOOBAS!"

OSI SOBECK

DEADLY DELAY

When the Jedi breach the Citadel and reach Piell, he tells them he gave half of the code for the Nexus Route to Captain Tarkin. Now the Jedi have to rescue Tarkin as well as Piell! This forces them to split up and slows them down. As they try to escape, the enemy catches up with them and prison guard Osi Sobeck unleashes a deadly pack of anoobas!

HOLO DATA

Even Piell is a small, aged Jedi from the planet Lannik. Piell lost an eye on an early mission, but it did not hold him back. He went on to become a long-serving member of the Council.

TRIUMPH IN TRAGEDY

Even in disaster, triumph can be found. The Jedi escape the anoobas, but Piell is fatally wounded by one of the vicious creatures. Before he dies, he passes on the secret data to Ahsoka. The rescue mission may have failed, but the vital routes are now in Jedi hands.

EYES HAVE LOW-LIGHT VISION

ALL NAUTOLANS HAVE 14 HEAD TENDRILS

WHAT HAPPENS WHEN KIT FISTO TAKES ON GENERAL GRIEVOUS?

He might seem relaxed and carefree, but Kit Fisto is one of the most formidable fighters in the entire Jedi Order. When he chances upon the lair of General Grievous, a battle between two of the greatest warriors in the galaxy seems inevitable. The only question is: Who will emerge as the victor?

Fallen Friend

Trapped in Grievous's base, Kit Fisto and Jedi Nahdar Vebb must stay cool if they are to get out alive. Vebb dies when he disobeys orders and tackles Grievous alone. Fisto, however, is too wise to let anger control his actions.

Desperate Duel

As the duel heats up, Fisto slices off Grievous's legs, forcing the cyborg to drag himself away for repairs. When he returns, Fisto sends him crashing to the floor with a huge Force push. Fisto will not finish off a helpless foe, however—it is against the Jedi Code. Soon Grievous's droids, the MagnaGuards, appear, and Fisto is left outnumbered.

Cool Getaway

Not many who stray into the lair of General Grievous escape in one piece; luckily Kit Fisto is prepared for sudden escapes. His loyal—though slightly nervous—astromech, R6-H5, is waiting to snatch his master to safety. They make a lightning getaway in the Jedi's starfighter.

45

WHICH IS THE DEADLIEST MONSTER THE JEDI HAVE FACED?

War is a deadly business, and occasionally its dangers come from unexpected sources—like these monstrous creatures. Sometimes, powerful beasts are turned into instruments of war against the Jedi, But which monster is the most fearsome? The competition is tough!

Scary Swamp Serpent

This stupendous snake with bone-crunching jaws lurks in the swamps of Nal Hutta and waits for prey to fall into its coils. Obi-Wan does exactly that while on the trail of Ziro the Hutt, but fortunately finds his lightsaber more than a match for the ravenous reptile.

Rampaging Roggwart

These monstrous meat-eaters have a savage nature and can be trained to work as watch-beasts—which is what General Grievous does with his nasty pet, Gor. The Jedi come face-to-face with the roggwart when they enter the general's lair on the Moon of Vassek. Despite Gor's power and body armor, Kit Fisto soon cuts him down to size.

Grim Gundark

With powerful jaws and a taste for blood, gundarks are one of the fiercest species in the galaxy and should be avoided at all costs! When Anakin and Obi-Wan come across one in a dark cave on Vanquor, they use the Force to bury it under boulders.

Gruesome Gutkurr

Tall, tough-shelled, insect-like creatures, the gutkurrs have armor that can withstand blaster fire. The Jedi encounter them on Ryloth, when a stampede of the beasts threatens to flatten a clone army. Obi-Wan uses the Force to tune into their primitive minds and redirects them to a canyon, where they can cause no more harm.

WHY DO SOME PEOPLE DISTRUST THE JEDI?

The Jedi are welcomed on countless worlds as champions of freedom and valiant defenders against Separatist invaders. Yet not everyone wants the Jedi on their planet . . .

CUT LAWQUANE

Lawquane is a clone deserter who settles with his Twi'lek wife on the planet Saleucami. He thinks clones should be free to live their own lives, and hopes to see out the Clone Wars as a quiet farmer, well away from Jedi eyes.

DUCHESS SATINE

Leader of the Mandalorians, the Duchess is also Head of the Council of Neutral Systems and a dear friend of Obi-Wan Kenobi. She believes in peace, and thinks the Jedi were wrong to become part of the Clone Wars.

THE LURMEN

The peaceful Lurmen are surprisingly tough, despite their small size and harmless looks. They are content to live their lives as humble farmers, and allow no weapons of any kind on their land. To them, the Jedi are bringers of war. They fear that the very presence of a Jedi in their village could bring on a Separatist attack.

CHAM SYNDULLA

Young Twi'lek noble Cham leads his freedom fighters in resisting the Separatist invasion of their world, Ryloth. Cham rejects help from the Jedi, telling them that having their army on his world would be just as bad as having the Separatists.

NUTE GUNRAY

Gunray is Viceroy of the Trade Federation. He and his people, the Neimoidians, have values that are at odds with the Jedi's. They are driven by a desire for riches and trust no one—especially the Jedi, who often stand in the way of their dishonest schemes.

WHY IS THE FREECO BIKE VITAL TO THE JEDI?

IT GLIDES

Using repulsorlift technology, the freeco bike glides above difficult terrains. This is ideal on Orto Plutonia, where the icy surface can ground any vehicle that touches it. The bike also glides over chasms in the ice that could send soldiers plummeting to their doom.

Not every mission is won by heavy hardware, and not every planet provides an ideal surface for tanks and walkers. The CK-6 swoop bike—also known as the freeco bike—is light and lacks big guns. But when the war makes its way to Orto Plutonia, the Jedi find that this speedy one-man craft is just what they need.

IT IS RIDER-FRIENDLY

Handy in a swift chase or retreat, the open-up cockpit means a rider can leap aboard in a split-second. Simple controls respond quickly to touch and allow them to be on their way in moments. A sliding windshield wards off the freezing wind and snow.

CK-6 SWOOP BIKE

The freeco is built for scouting terrain. This version is adapted for icy conditions with extra cockpit heating and micro-defrost coils in the screen.

- **SPEED** 440 KPH (273 MPH)
- **WEAPONS** TWIN LASER CANNONS

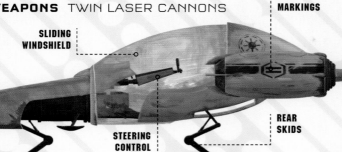

SLIDING WINDSHIELD

UNIT MARKINGS

STEERING CONTROL

REAR SKIDS

IT MAKES TEAMWORK EASY

Agile and sleek, the freeco bike is perfect for riding in a close pack. Collision sensors help riders avoid hitting each other. Bikes are highly maneuverable, enabling bikers surrounded by the enemy to form an instant defensive circle.

WHICH JEDI DO THE SITH FEAR THE MOST?

For the Sith and the Separatists, the very word "Jedi" is breathed with immense hatred. However, they also fear all Jedi, and among their eternal enemies are three notorious Jedi who inspire a greater amount of dread than any others.

Amazing Mace

Stern, passionate, and direct, Mace is at the center of all Jedi operations. On the planet Ryloth, he destroys a squad of droids almost single-handedly. As a result, the city is freed from Separatist occupation.

Powerful Plo Koon

Plo Koon is a formidable Jedi who wears a mask to breathe because oxygen harms him. Known for his grim outlook and strong sense of justice, Koon serves as a lifetime member of the Jedi Council. He is an ace starfighter pilot, and the Separatist fleet dread the sight of his squadron emerging from hyperspace.

HOLO DATA

Mace Windu is a male Jedi from Haruun Kal. He uses a violet-bladed lightsaber and fights in the Vaapad style, which channels powerful emotions. Mace believes in fighting only as a last resort.

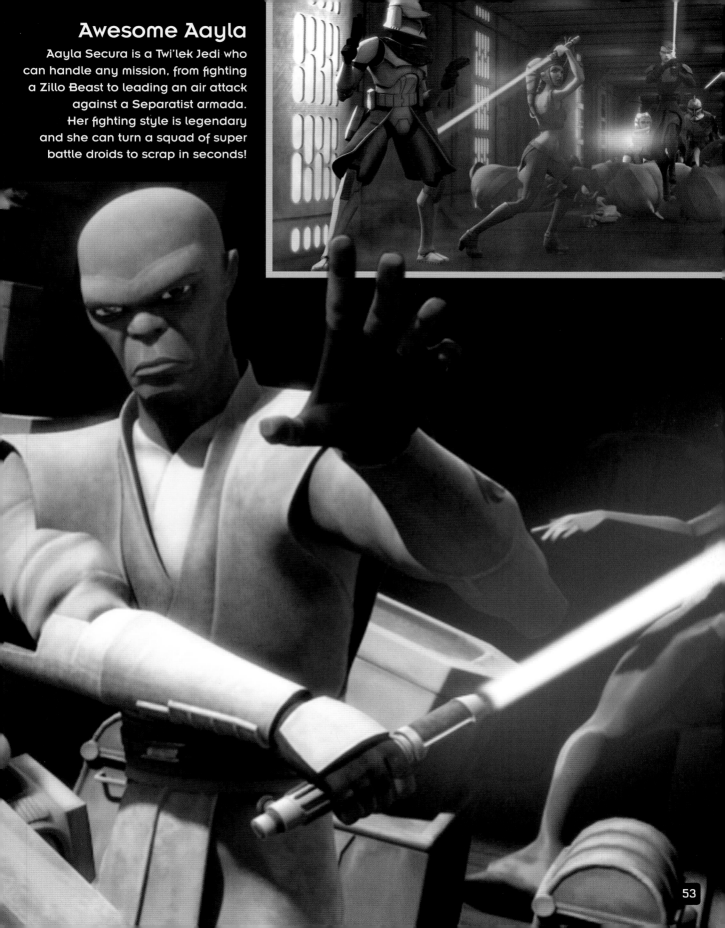

Awesome Aayla

Aayla Secura is a Twi'lek Jedi who can handle any mission, from fighting a Zillo Beast to leading an air attack against a Separatist armada. Her fighting style is legendary and she can turn a squad of super battle droids to scrap in seconds!

THINKING BIG

While on a mission under the seas of Kamino, Obi-Wan finds himself surrounded by enemy aqua droids. With his own transport destroyed, he hitches a ride on a flying sea creature called an aiwha. Without specialist training, only a true master of the Force would attempt such a feat.

BUZZING OFF

Anakin decides it is better to take flight than risk capture during a battle with Asajj Ventress on top of a monastery on the planet Teth. He uses the Force to turn one of the local giant flying insects into a useful steed.

WHAT IS THE
CRAZIEST

Fighting a relentless war on many alien worlds can land a Jedi in some tricky situations. There isn't always a trusty droid or handy Padawan to help you out of a tight corner! So Jedi have learned to use the Force and their instincts to find ways out of trouble that might seem a little bizarre.

HOLO DATA

The aiwha is a gigantic beast whose huge wings can either be used to swim in water or fly through the air. They are found only on the planets Kamino and Naboo.

ROCKETING AWAY

Anakin finds a daring form of emergency transport while fighting the Separatists in the Outer Rim. He jumps on board a Separatist rocket droid and uses it to plunge through enemy lines.

JEDI ESCAPE?

RIDING A REPTILE

When he needs to make a quick getaway on the planet Zygerria, Obi-Wan uses the Force to help him ride on one of the planet's enormous gliding lizards.

CAN A BOUNTY HUNTER DEFEAT A JEDI?

It's hard to imagine a mere criminal besting a Jedi. Yet the war has created a grim underworld where many will try their luck. The feared bounty hunter Cad Bane is happy to take on a Jedi Knight—as long as the odds are stacked in his favor!

HOLO DATA

Hailing from the Inner Rim world of Patrolia, Robonino is a regular crony of Cad Bane. Small in stature, this blue bandit has an aquatic appearance, with fins and a tail.

With Careful Planning

Bane has been paid to free Ziro the Hutt from prison. His plan is to take senators hostage and exchange one of them for Ziro. After acquiring plans to the Senate building, he seals the area and jams all communications. Nothing is left to chance until he has the means to free Ziro.

With Back-up

A plan like this could go wrong in a dozen ways, so Bane makes sure to keep an ace up his sleeve. He brings along Aurra Sing, a super sniper, to take out any unexpected opposition. Aurra is a cold-blooded mercenary, just like Bane. It's no wonder he feels right at home in her company!

With Allies

To help his plan succeed, Bane enlists a team of the most talented lowlifes in the galaxy. His secret weapon, Robonino, is small in size, but big in impact. While Anakin is distracted by the other bounty hunters, Robonino zaps him from behind with an electric shocker device.

With Gadgets

Bane uses a laser web to trap Anakin and his hostages until he makes his getaway. They cannot get through it alive, but Anakin manages to cut a route to freedom—through the floor.

HIDDEN HERO

Dressed in a hooded robe, Ahsoka pretends to be a servant in order to sneak onto a Separatist command ship above the planet Pantora. Once aboard, her disguise helps her to remain undetected as she solves a kidnapping mystery, rescues a hostage, and foils a plot to force Pantora to join the Separatist cause.

DO JEDI EVER USE SPIES?

Bending the truth may not strictly be the Jedi way, but sometimes it can be helpful—especially in times of war. Discovering enemy secrets is vital, and spying becomes a necessary art. At times a Jedi must hide their true identity to enter enemy territory, and pretend in order to uncover the deadly secrets of their evil foes.

ANAKIN THE SLAVER

On the planet Zygerria, Anakin poses as a rich slaver to find out why a whole colony of Togrutas has vanished. With Ahsoka disguised as his slave, Anakin becomes a favorite of the Zygerrian queen—and discovers a plan to turn the peaceful Togrutas into an army of slaves.

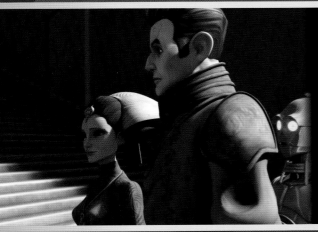

SENATOR SPY

Yoda asks Padmé Amidala to use her old friendship with a senator in order to spy for the Jedi. Padmé's mission is to accompany the senator to an important meeting with the Neimoidians, who are known Separatist supporters. Padmé soon uncovers a plot to build a new droid factory on Geonosis and recounts the details of the scheme to Anakin—who is also there disguised as Padmé's pilot!

THE SPY WITHIN

Sometimes the Jedi find themselves spied upon. Boba Fett is the son of bounty hunter Jango Fett, whose cells were used to create clone troopers, so he looks just like all the clone recruits. Boba poses as one so he can try to get close to, and then assassinate Mace Windu, who defeated his father.

WHICH SPACECRAFT ARE VITAL TO THE JEDI?

As the Separatist onslaught extends across the galaxy, the Jedi must reach battle zones as quickly as possible and deliver the right kind of response when they get there. Whether for a massive land battle or a small-scale secret mission, certain trusted craft have emerged as firm Jedi favorites.

JEDI CRUISER

When the Jedi need to ship out an army big enough to retake a planet from the enemy, they call on the heavyweight Jedi cruiser. Each of these huge vessels is commanded by a Jedi general and carries an experienced Republic admiral.

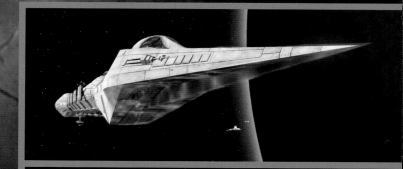

STEALTH SHIP

The Jedi stealth ship is able to enter enemy space unnoticed. Cloaking technology creates a field around the ship that makes it invisible to sensors. Perfect for spying, secret troop landings, and breaking blockades, this ship is a secret that must not fall into enemy hands!

JEDI CRUISER

This colossal destroyer can carry more than 400 fighter craft. Its main strike power comes from eight dual turbolasers.

- **LENGTH** 1,137 M (3,729 FT)
- **CREW** 7,400 CLONE TROOPERS
- **WEAPONS** TURBOLASERS, PROTON TORPEDOES, LASER CANNONS

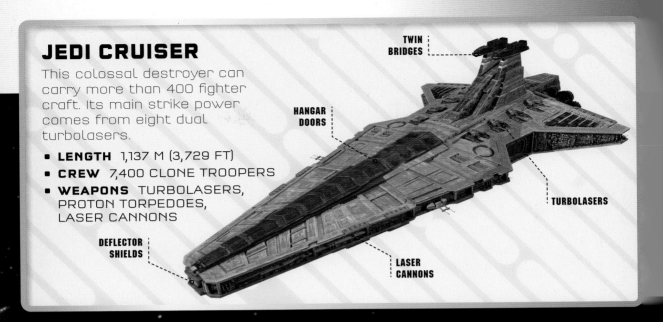

TWIN BRIDGES

HANGAR DOORS

TURBOLASERS

LASER CANNONS

DEFLECTOR SHIELDS

Y-WING FIGHTER

The Y-wing is swift and carries a heavy payload of explosives, making it ideal for bombing raids where ground forces need urgent assistance. Armed with ion cannons, laser cannons, and proton torpedoes, it can also bring down craft much larger than itself.

V-19 TORRENT

High speeds and adjustable wings enable the V-19 to pull off tricky maneuvers. Armed with mis launchers, it can damage enemy vessels sever times its size. Heavy armor makes it ideal for defending Republic forces in enemy territory.

HOW DO THE JEDI WEAKEN THEIR

The Jedi spend much of the war repelling the attacks of their enemies. But suppose they were able to weaken them so they could not launch an attack in the first place? When the Jedi discover plans to build a droid mill on Geonosis, they come up with a brilliant strategy. First, they will take apart the droid mill's defenses. Then they will move in to destroy the mill!

THEY DEPLOY

First, gunships descend on Geonosis to land assault troops. Next, Y-wing bombers sweep in to destroy the Geonosian cannons. Then a Jedi-led squad takes out the enemy scanners. At this point, AT-TE tanks are able to move in and blow up the shield generator, leaving the mill open to the final stage of the attack.

ENEMIES?

THEY PLAN

The Jedi use the Holonet to study the defenses on Geonosis. They consult the far-away Jedi Council via signals traveling through hyperspace. They decide on a three-pronged land attack on the mill's shield generator.

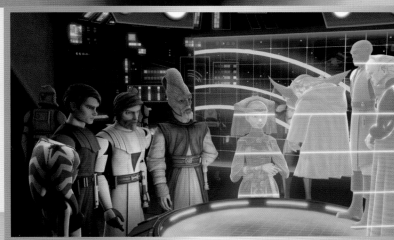

HOLO DATA

Geonosis lies in the Outer Rim. It is ruled by Poggle the Lesser, an ally of Count Dooku. A key world in the Clone Wars, it has supplied many droids for the Separatist army.

THEY DESTROY

Anakin lures enemy super tanks onto the mill's main bridge and destroys it, taking out the mill's last line of defense. Then Ahsoka and Barriss Offee sneak through underground catacombs to sabotage the main reactor. The mill is destroyed!

CAN A JEDI DEFEAT A

In the ruins of a temple on the planet Geonosis, the Jedi discover a nest of undead Geonosians. The zombies threaten to spread across the galaxy. Do the Jedi have the power to stop them?

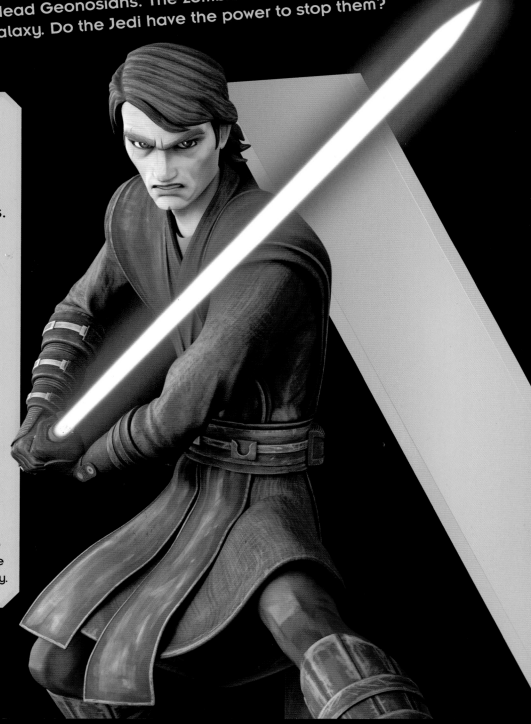

JEDI STRENGTHS

A Jedi has enough going for him or her to handle most foes.

1 Lightsaber: Powerful enough to slice up an undead foe.

2 Force push: A Jedi strong in the Force can slam a zombie against a rock wall with one push.

3 Fighting skills: Superior hand-to-hand battle training.

4 Force leap: Jedi can use this to make evasive or attacking jumps.

5 Tactical mind: Jedi will choose the right time and place to tackle foes.

6 Superior tech: Jedi use powerful lights to blind the zombies, leading to victory.

ZOMBIE STRENGTHS

Being dead already makes them hard to finish off!

1 Indestructible: Zombies can survive losing limbs and even their heads, and are unable to feel pain.

2 Collective mind: Geonosians have a single, hive mind, so they have perfect teamwork skills.

3 Dark-adapted vision: Unlike their Jedi foes, zombies are able to see well in dark tunnels.

4 Numbers: They can swamp opponents with overwhelming force.

5 Temple home: Their superior knowledge of the temple labyrinth gives them many ways to attack.

6 Fear factor: Their frightening look strikes terror and panic into foes.

ZOMBIE?

CAN PADAWANS SUCCEED WITHOUT THEIR MASTERS?

MIRIALAN INITIATE TATTOOS

SIMILAR STYLE LIGHTSABER TO LUMINARA

HOLO DATA

Barriss Offee is a female Padawan of the Mirialan species. She has diamond-shaped tattoos on her face and hands which, in Mirialan culture, show she is an initiate—a student of the Force.

During a Padawan's training to become a Jedi, their Master is almost always there to guide them. It is a Padawan's role to watch their Master and learn. But in the heat of war, they may have to fight alone. To succeed, a Padawan must draw upon the lessons already learned at the Jedi Temple.

WHO IS BARRISS?

Barriss is a studious Padawan and a gifted healer. Under her Master, Luminara Unduli, she has learned to control her feelings, making her cool in any crisis. In battle, she prefers to use her lightsaber for defense rather than attack, using the Soresu style.

They Have Been Taught To Fight

Padawans have been taught to master the Force and not to be overwhelmed by anger. Ahsoka and Barriss can summon all they have learned and use it cooly under fire.

They Are Well-Prepared

No Padawan is sent into danger without guidance. When Barriss Offee sneaks into a droid factory, her Master has helped by instructing her to memorize the junctions in the secret passages below their target.

They Are Not Truly Alone

The best-laid plans can still go wrong, but Padawans need not despair. The unique bond between a Master and their Padawan can aid them. When Ahsoka and Barriss are lost in battle and almost given up for dead, Anakin and Luminara sense their presence using the Force and rescue them.

CAN THE JEDI EVER ALLY WITH BOUNTY

JEDI ALLY RATING

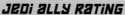 

SUGI

Sugi is the leader of the group. Not a typical bounty hunter, she considers herself honorable and is proud of her work. She demands respect—and gets it. Later in the war, Sugi teams up with Ahsoka against Trandoshan hunters.

RACE: Zabrak (homeworld: Iridonia)

SKILL: Hand-to-hand combat, vibroblade master, marksman, tactician, talented pilot

WEAPONS: Vibroblade, EE-3 blaster rifle

JEDI ALLY RATING

EMBO

Embo is a ruthless and experienced assassin. During the pirate attack, Embo is quick to seek out the enemy and silences a pirate scout. When the scout fails to return, the pirates are alerted to the fact that they face tough opposition.

RACE: Kyuzo (homeworld: Phatrong)

SKILLS: Expert in unarmed combat, can leap great distances, powerful and accurate thrower of his trademark shield-hat

WEAPONS: Shield-hat and bowcaster

HUNTERS?

Bounty hunters typically take jobs for credits, not for moral reasons. But on some missions they can find themselves serving as forces for good. On Felucia, the Jedi discover a group of bounty hunters who are defending local farmers from pirates, so the Jedi decide to help them complete their task.

JEDI ALLY RATING

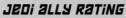

RUMI PARAMITA

A daring mercenary, Rumi is not afraid to be the first into action—but that tactic can sometimes backfire. During the battle with the pirates, Rumi is struck down by enemy cannon fire.

RACE: Frenk (homeworld: Gorebei)

SKILLS: Battle tactics, unarmed combat, expert sniper

WEAPONS: Chrome blaster pistol, IQA-11 blaster rifle

JEDI ALLY RATING

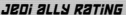

SERIPAS

A being of tiny size, Seripas has become a formidable figure thanks to a towering robotic suit of his own creation. While in action against the pirates, Seripas is crushed by a giant fungus and Ahsoka saves him.

RACE: Unknown

SKILLS: Armor and weapons design, robotic suit control, close combat

WEAPONS: Suit has built-in blasters and gives enhanced strength

YELLOW KIFFAR FACE TATTOO

LIGHTSABER READY FOR ATARU COMBAT

He Speaks His Mind

Quinlan's habit of saying what he thinks can land him in trouble. When he accuses the Hutt Council of helping Ziro the Hutt escape from prison, Quinlan gets out alive only because he has Obi-Wan with him.

WHAT MAKES QUINLAN VOS THE WILDEST JEDI?

Jedi are expected to be cool and reserved, keeping their feelings to themselves at all times. With a look all his own and an attitude to match, Quinlan Vos is none of these things. Quinlan may be the Jedi wild card—but it is a useful one to have in the pack.

WHO IS QUINLAN?

Quinlan is a Jedi with a troubled past. He has only recently returned to the Jedi after succumbing to the dark side of the Force. A rare Force ability called psychometry allows Quinlan to pick up memories from objects that he touches.

He Gets Into Trouble

A dislike of rules leads Quinlan into trouble on a regular basis—and he often takes his friends with him! When he and Obi-Wan track Ziro the Hutt through the desert, Quinlan refuses to bring droids. Without the benefit of droid sensors, the Jedi walk right into the clutches of a desert serpent, with Obi-Wan barely escaping in one piece.

He Takes Chances

Quinlan just loves to take crazy chances! Even when up against the deadliest bounty hunter around, Cad Bane, he hurls himself into a life-and-death mid-air battle with no thought for his own safety. Luckily, Quinlan's do-or-die attitude pays off, and he scores a victory.

TRUE OR FALSE?
Quinlan Vos saves Obi-Wan's life.

True. Quinlan saves Obi-Wan from Cad Bane.

WHY IS VENTRESS

With her pale skin, shadowy eyes, and hairless head, Asajj Ventress is one of the most striking figures of the Clone Wars. Count Dooku's trusted assassin frequently stands between the Jedi and the success of important missions. So why don't they just defeat her once and for all? Ventress has a rare blend of skills that even the Jedi cannot sweep aside.

SHE IS STRONG WITH THE FORCE

Ventress has more weaponry than lightsabers at her disposal. When they aren't enough to beat an opponent, Ventress uses the Force. As a child, Ventress was trained by a Jedi before falling under the influence of Count Dooku, so she has Force power to spare. She can even lift and choke two Jedi at once!

SHE USES TWO LIGHTSABERS

Fighting with two lightsabers at once takes expert skill. Using this fighting style, which is known as Jar'Kai, enables Ventress to defend and attack at the same time. This is especially useful when facing Jedi, who often work in pairs.

TOUGH TO BEAT?

"I WILL DESTROY THE JEDI!"
ASAJJ VENTRESS

SHE PLANS AHEAD
When Ventress plans a dangerous mission, she also plans her way out of it! Anakin comes close to beating her in a battle on the planet Kamino, but she has an escape ship on hand to help her make a swift exit.

WHO ARE THE FORCE-WIELDERS?

When Anakin answers a distress call using a Jedi code that is 2,000 years old, he finds himself in a world outside of time. The three Force-wielders who live there seem able to perform miracles, change their shape, and control minds. What can they want with Anakin?

HOLO DATA

Force-wielders are also known as the Ones. It is thought that they descend from a race called the Celestials. Mortis is their adopted world, but their original home is unknown.

They Live On Mortis

The Force-wielders' home planet of Mortis seems to disobey natural laws. Islands of rock float in the sky and day changes to night in an instant. Anything is possible there, because the planet is made from the Force and reflects the minds of the Force-wielders who live upon it.

They Are At War

The magical landscapes of Mortis hide a grim secret—it is a world at eternal war. The Father of the Force-wielders is old and wise, but his children are in conflict. The Son has been taken over by the dark side of the Force, while the Daughter fights for peace. If the dark side wins, the galaxy could be threatened.

They Want Anakin

The Father holds the balance of power between the Son and the Daughter, but he is coming to the end of his days. The Father wants Anakin to take over his rule and keep his increasingly dangerous Son in check, but it is an honor the Jedi does not want.

WHAT IS A FORCE SPIRIT?

Over time, phantom figures of Jedi have been seen in the galaxy. These Force spirits are the presences of Jedi who have long since passed on, appearing to their living comrades at times of crisis. But how can such a thing be? The Force holds many mysteries . . .

One Of The Wisest Jedi

The power to appear as a Force spirit is extremely rare. Only Jedi who have become experts in the Living Force can remain as spirits in death. Jedi Master Qui-Gon Jinn became a Force spirit, and Yoda and Obi-Wan learn from him to do the same.

A Messenger

A Force spirit appears at a time of great change in the galaxy, and can bring warnings to the living. Qui-Gon appears to Anakin on the planet Mortis, where the dark side of the Force is at its strongest. He warns Anakin that he is in danger from the dark side, and directs him to the Well of the Dark Side to learn about his future.

Part Of The Force

Qui-Gon Jinn was lost before the Clone Wars began, but he appears as a Force spirit during that time. When he died, Qui-Gon managed to join with the Force, but he kept his own spirit and essence. Now, at certain times, he can return to the land of the living.

TRUE OR FALSE?
Qui-Gon was once Padawan to Count Dooku.

True—before Dooku fell to the dark side.

WHO IS QUI-GON?

Qui-Gon Jinn was a wise Jedi Master and mentor to Obi-Wan Kenobi. His appearance as a Force spirit on Mortis during the Clone Wars is testament to his skills in the ways of the Living Force when he was alive. He died in a battle with Darth Maul on the planet Naboo.

WHAT HAPPENS WHEN JEDI FIGHTS

The Jedi are trained to fight a wide range of foes. But what happens when they face that most unexpected of opponents—another Jedi? Ahsoka is Anakin's Padawan. He has taught her every trick he knows. When dark forces turn Ahsoka against Anakin, how will the Master handle the Padawan?

FRIENDS BECOME ENEMIES

This battle would not normally happen. The Jedi do not fight among themselves—it is not the Jedi way. But when Ahsoka is taken over by the dark side of the Force, it makes her want to strike out at her Master.

JEDI?

"I DON'T NEED YOU ANY MORE!"
AHSOKA TANO

HOLO DATA
Ahsoka is overwhelmed by the dark side on Mortis, a planet where the Force is at its strongest. A powerful being called the Son hopes to use her to drive Anakin to the dark side.

TOO MUCH KNOWLEDGE
The battle with Ahsoka is not an easy one for Anakin. As Ahsoka is his Padawan, she is very familiar with his fighting style. Anakin also realizes that she is not herself, and has no desire to harm her. The situation gives Ahsoka the edge, and at one point she even disarms her Master.

SOMETHING GIVES
Obi-Wan Kenobi helps Anakin end the duel without anybody being hurt. Using the Force, Anakin draws out the dark side within Ahsoka, and she soon returns to her true self.

79

Kalifa's Anger

A human from Corellia, Kalifa is leader of the three younglings on Island 4 and the most powerful. In order to stop one of the Trandoshan hunters, Kalifa lifts him from the ground and strangles him with a Force choke. It would have been the end for the enemy if Ahsoka hadn't stepped in to break Kalifa's deadly hold.

Young Ahsoka

Ahsoka is now a Jedi Padawan, but she was once a youngling. Ahsoka revealed great power as a youngster and was trained in the Force by Yoda. In lightsaber combat, Ahsoka would regularly beat older students!

HOW POWERFUL ARE JEDI YOUNGLINGS?

Younglings are the Jedi of the future. They are not ready to become Padawans, but are old enough to have started learning to use the Force. On Island 4, a trio of youngsters are being hunted for sport by evil Trandoshans. When Ahsoka joins them, she learns just how powerful younglings can be.

TRUE OR FALSE?

Cad Bane once babysat for Jedi younglings.

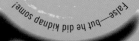

False—but he did kidnap some!

Speedy O-Mer

O-Mer is perhaps the weakest of the trio, and survives by using Force leaps to escape harm. However, when the younglings escape from the island, the young Cerean shows skill and bravery in flying a Trandoshan speeder into the middle of his foes.

Tricky Jinx

Twi'lek youngling Jinx has a growing ability in the Force, making him a youngling full of surprises. Jinx has a powerful Force push—a useful weapon in combat against the Trandoshan hunters. He can even perform the difficult Jedi mind-trick of bending his enemy's thoughts and making them say things they don't mean to!

WHO CAN DEFEAT A JEDI?

Honor, glory, adventure—being a Jedi can bring many rewards, though they seek them not. But it brings perils, too. Dark forces see the Jedi Order as an obstacle to be swept away. And while the Jedi are strong, some of their foes can be relentless . . .

Vengeful Clones

The clone troopers of the 501st had to turn on their leader, Jedi Pong Krell, when he was overcome by the dark side of the Force. They lured him into the clutches of a killer plant, then captured him when he was weak from fighting it.

Grisly Grievous

This merciless general has destroyed many Jedi, including Nahdar Vebb, who foolishly took him on in his own lair. Cyborg upgrades turned Grievous from a reptilian warrior into one of the most feared figures in the galaxy.

Sinister Savage

The monstrous Savage Opress was created by the Nightsisters on the planet Dathomir and trained by Count Dooku himself. On his very first mission, he slays the Roonen Jedi Master Halsey, along with his Padawan Knox, in a brief but brutal battle. Savage is keen to impress his new Master with his power and ruthlessness.

DOUBLE UP

Ahsoka has to battle Separatist droids while being thrown about by the Mon Cala seas. She opts to fight using twin lightsabers. They give her more balance and control in the water and make her twice as dangerous.

CAN A JEDI FIGHT

Be prepared for anything—that's one lesson the Jedi know very well! On the sea planet of Mon Cala, Count Dooku is plotting the downfall of peace-loving Prince Lee-Char. When the Jedi step in to help the Prince, Dooku thinks they will be easy to defeat on the unfamiliar, watery world. But Jedi are very quick to adapt . . .

"I THINK I'D LIKE TO GO FOR A SWIM."

OBI-WAN KENOBI

HOLO DATA

A regular lightsaber does not work under water, so Jedi operating on sea planets like Mon Cala modify their blades. All the Jedi sent to Mon Cala use these special underwater blades.

SPECIAL TACTICS

Anakin knows he cannot move as quickly in water as on land, so he fights the enemy at close-range where he can make every blow count. He also takes advantage of his watery surroundings, escaping from enemy droids by clinging to sinking spaceship wreckage.

UNDERWATER?

BE PREPARED

Obi-Wan Kenobi always expects the unexpected, so he takes a specially adapted underwater lightsaber to Kamino. When he comes across enemy aqua droids in the Kamino ocean, he is equipped to slice his way out of trouble.

CAN A JEDI TURN EVIL?

As the Clone Wars go on with no sign of victory for the Jedi, some fall victim to despair. Pong Krell, a respected and powerful Jedi Knight, sees a dark vision of his Order being destroyed by its foes. It leads Krell to make a grim decision: If the enemy are going to win, why not join them?

THROUGH TEMPTATION

The dark side is strong and seductive. Krell starts to crave its power and hopes to become a Sith apprentice.

THROUGH SPITE

To assist the enemy, Krell sabotages Jedi battle plans. When his clone troopers question his decisions, he tricks them into attacking each other.

THROUGH PASSION

Giving in to a new passion for violence, Krell cracks and reveals he has changed sides. He turns on his own men and tries to destroy them all.

WHO SHOT

PAINFUL MISSION

Anakin and Ahsoka are with Obi-Wan on the night he is gunned down. When Ahsoka discovers the fallen Jedi, there are no signs of life. Setting aside their grief, Anakin and Ahsoka waste no time in hunting down Rako Hardeen—the criminal they believe to be responsible for their mentor's death.

OBI-WAN KENOBI?

One of the greatest Jedi of all, Obi-Wan Kenobi, is felled by a single sniper on the planet Coruscant. The suspected marksman is swiftly captured, but many questions hang over this shocking event. What dark forces are behind the attack? Why didn't Kenobi save himself, as he has so often before? And what is the true story behind his mysterious assassin?

THE SUSPECT

Rako Hardeen is a bounty hunter known for his skill with a sniper rifle. He is caught shortly after the shooting in a seedy city bar, where he has been celebrating the death of a Jedi.

"HEADING DOWN A DARK PATH, WE ARE."

YODA

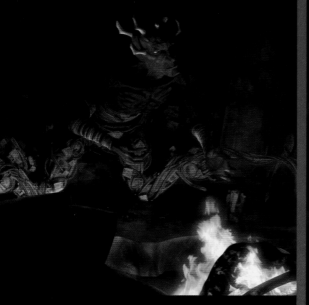

HE IS FOUND . . .

Savage Opress, aided by the Nightsisters, finds his brother, Darth Maul, in a cave on the junk world of Lotho Minor. Now a mad creature with self-constructed, spidery robot legs, Maul is taken back to Dathomir.

HE IS REBUILT . . .

The sorcery of the Nightsisters rebuilds Maul with improved humanoid legs, made from pieces of old super battle droids. They also piece together Maul's disturbed mind, to the best of their power.

HOW DOES DARTH MAUL RETURN TO PLAGUE THE JEDI?

For many years, Darth Maul was thought to be dead after he was cut in two during his duel with Obi-Wan Kenobi. But it seems he survived, kept alive by his dark willpower alone. Now he has revenge in his sights.

SO BEGINS HIS
REVENGE!

GLOSSARY

ASTROMECH DROID
A robot designed to repair and help navigate starships.

BATTLE DROID
A Separatist robot designed for combat.

BOUNTY HUNTER
Someone who is paid to capture or destroy wanted people.

CHANCELLOR
The title given to the head of the Republic.

CHOSEN ONE
A person spoken of in an old Jedi prophesy, who will restore balance to the Force.

CLONE TROOPERS
Republic soldiers who are identical because they all share the same genes.

CREDITS
Metal coins or chips used as currency.

CYBORG
A being who is part robot and part living organism.

DARK SIDE
The evil side of the Force that feeds off negative emotions.

DROID
A robot. Droids come in many shapes and sizes and perform a variety of duties.

THE FORCE
A mysterious energy that flows through the galaxy and all living things.

FORCE LEAP
A huge jump made by somebody using the Force to enhance their natural ability

FORCE LIGHTNING
Lethal rays of blue energy used as a weapon.

FORCE PUSH
A blast of energy that a Force user can use to knock over an opponent.

GALACTIC BASIC
The most widely spoken language in the Galaxy.

GRAND ARMY
A branch of the Republic army made up entirely of clone troopers. It is led by Jedi officers.

GUNGANS
An amphibious species from the planet Naboo.

HOLONET
A communications network that enables instant contact between Republic planets all over the galaxy.

HYPERDRIVE
A propulsion system that enables a spacecraft to launch into hyperspace.

HYPERSPACE
A dimension in space where starships can travel at super-fast speeds.

ION CANNON
A weapon that fires ionized particles to disable vehicles or equipment.
. . . .

JEDI
A member of the Jedi Order. Jedi follow the peace-loving light side of the Force.
. . . .

JEDI HIGH COUNCIL
Twelve senior Jedi who meet to make important decisions.
. . . .

JEDI KNIGHT
A full member of the Jedi Order who has completed all of their Jedi training.
. . . .

JEDI MASTER
An experienced and powerful Jedi who is training a Padawan.
. . . .

JEDI ORDER
An ancient organization that promotes peace and justice throughout the galaxy.
. . . .

JEDI TEMPLE
The headquarters of the Jedi Order, situated on the planet Coruscant.
. . . .

LIGHT SIDE
The good side of the Force that brings peace and justice.
. . . .

LIGHTSABER
A sword-like weapon with a blade of pure energy that is used by Jedi and Sith.
. . . .

MAGNAGUARDS
Advanced battle droids used by General Grievous as bodyguards.
. . . .

MERCENARY
Someone who fights for payment rather than for a cause.
. . . .

NEIMOIDIANS
A sneaky, money-loving species who control the Trade Federation.
. . . .

NIGHTSISTERS
A clan of witches who use the Force in their dark magic.
. . . .

PADAWAN
A Jedi apprentice who is being trained by a Jedi Master.
. . . .

PLASMA
A gas-like substance made from electrically charged particles.
. . . .

PROTOCOL DROID
A droid designed to help relations between different beings run smoothly.
. . . .

REPUBLIC
The democratic government that rules many planets in the galaxy.
. . . .

REPULSORLIFT
Anti-gravity technology designed for lifting objects.
. . . .

SENATE
The government of the Republic. It is made up of senators from all over the galaxy.
. . . . . .

SENATOR
Somone who acts as a representative for their planet in the Senate.
. . . .

SEPARATISTS
An alliance of those who are opposed to the Republic.
. . . .

SITH
An ancient sect of Force-sensitives who seek to use the dark side of the Force to gain power.
. . . .

SITH APPRENTICE
A Sith who is being trained in the dark side of the Force by a Sith Master.
. . . .

SITH MASTER
An experienced and powerful Sith who is training an apprentice.
. . . .

STARFIGHTER
A small, fast, highly maneuverable spacecraft designed for battle.
. . . .

TECHNO UNION
A collection of firms who produce droids, spacecraft, and arms to sell to the Separatists.
. . . .

TRACTOR BEAM
A beam that can grab and draw objects toward its source.
. . . .

TRADE FEDERATION
An organization that controls most of the trade and commerce in the galaxy.
. . . .

TURBOLASER
A large and extremely powerful laser cannon.
. . . .

WOOKIEES
A hairy species from the forest planet of Kashyyyk.
. . . .

YOUNGLING
A Force-sensitive child who is being trained by the Jedi and may one day become a Padawan.
. . . .

INDEX

Characters are listed under their most frequently used common name, for example Anakin Skywalker is found under "A" and "Darth Maul" is under "D."

For Dorling Kindersley

Editors Pamela Afram, Julia March
Project Editor Hannah Dolan
Designers Nick Avery, Mark Richards
Project Art Editor Clive Savage
Managing Editor Laura Gilbert
Design Manager Maxine Pedliham
Art Director Ron Stobbart
Publisher Simon Beecroft
Publishing Director Alex Allan
Pre-Production Producer Siu Yin Chan
Senior Producer Shabana Shakir

For Lucasfilm

Executive Editor J. W. Rinzler
Art Director Troy Alders
Keeper of the Holocron Leland Chee
Director of Publishing Carol Roeder

The publisher would like to thank the following for
their kind permission to reproduce their photograph:
pp.38–39 Dreamstime.com: Snokid (background).

Published in the United States in 2013 by DK Publishing
375 Hudson Street, New York, New York 10014

10 9 8 7 6 5 4 3 2 1
001—184092—Jan/13

A catalog record for this book is available
from the Library of Congress.

ISBN: 978-0-7566-9795-2

Color reproduction by Alta Image, UK
Printed and bound by Hung Hing, China

Discover more at
www.dk.com
www.starwars.com